# 1

# Every king's bad dream

King Codger shook with terror. He
peered over the edge of the cliff.
All he could see was a cloud of white
spray. All he could hear was the roar
and crash of falling water.

Behind him, the sound of a nasty
voice was getting nearer and nearer.

'Help! Help!' squeaked King Codger. 'Somebody help!'

Outside the king's bedroom, Grizzle, the king's trusty servant, sighed and put down the breakfast tray he was carrying.

The king was having one of his bad dreams.

'I'm coming, Your Highness,' he muttered.

At the bottom of the king's enormous bed, a mound of bedclothes twisted and rolled like a sack full of snakes.

Grizzle poured out a cup of tea. Then he lifted up a corner of the royal sheet.

A long, whiskery face, like an old parsnip, looked up at him.

'Ah, Grizzle, it's you,' gasped King Codger. 'For a moment ...' His head fell back on the pillows.

Poor King Codger. It was always the same bad dream.

His daughter, Wolverina, was chasing him. She was yelling at the top of her voice.

'It's mine! It's mine! Give it! Or else!'

King Codger pulled the bedclothes over his head.

'It's your own fault, Sire,' said Grizzle, who knew all about the king's bad dreams. He stirred ten spoonfuls of sugar into the royal tea mug. 'You should never have told the princesses you were going to retire to the seaside.'

'But I thought Wolverina would be happy to share the kingdom with her sister,' moaned King Codger.

Grizzle made a rude noise. 'Since when has the Lady Wolverina shared anything?'

King Codger closed his eyes. His
daughters floated in front of him.

The oldest was called Goldie-Ox. She
was just like his dear departed wife:
blonde as a haystack, friendly as a
kitten, and wide as a drawbridge.

The king frowned. Perhaps she was a
bit too friendly. The last time she had
hugged him, she nearly cracked his ribs.

GOLDIE-OX

And then there was his other daughter, Wolverina. She wasn't like anyone in the family. In fact, Wolverina wasn't like anyone he had ever met – including trolls, goblins and ogres.

Wolverina was bony as a vulture. And as for her nature – the king shuddered. She was just like a wolverine: cunning, bad-tempered, and she had a nasty bite if she didn't get her own way.

WOLVERINA

9

King Codger sighed. If only his dear, departed wife hadn't gone dragon-hunting, and taken an umbrella instead of a sword by mistake. 'She'd know what to do,' he muttered to himself, 'if she was still here.'

'I beg your pardon, Sire,' said Grizzle. He laid out a matching tunic and cloak in blue satin with fake leopardskin trim. Despite his troubles, King Codger was always a snappy dresser.

'My wife, Queen Hundridwate, did make me promise to share my kingdom equally,' replied the king. 'They were her last words.' He blushed. 'Apart from the ones addressed to the person who put the umbrella stand in the wrong place.'

'And who could forget them?' thought Grizzle to himself. Even Spangle, the court magician, had never heard anything like it.

And he knew countless oaths uttered by badly-behaved witches.

At that moment, a flash of inspiration hit Grizzle and he almost dropped the crown he was polishing.

'Call for Spangle!' cried Grizzle, trying not to sound too pleased with himself. 'It's about time he stopped fooling around with frogs and princesses.'

'Grizzle, you're a genius!'

King Codger leapt out of bed and jumped about the room as if he had ants in his pants. 'Call for the Ladies Goldie-Ox and Wolverina! We shall settle the future of the kingdom once and for all!'

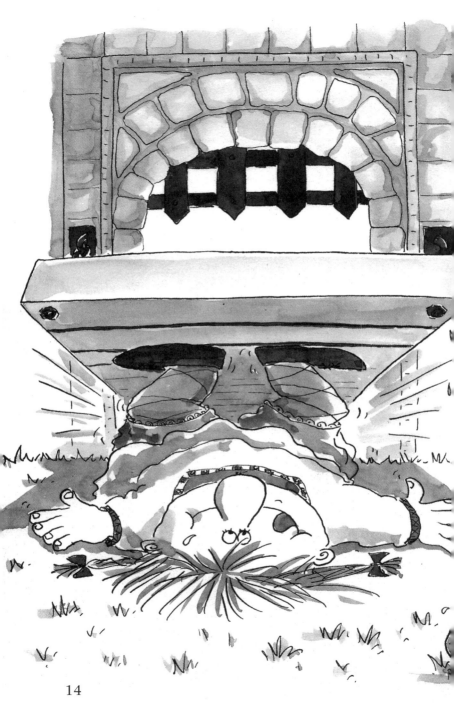

# 2

# A dog in the manger

'And-a-one,' puffed Goldie-Ox. 'And-a-two. And-a-three. Hup!'

The Lady Goldie-Ox lay on her back and straightened her knees. The palace drawbridge rose slowly from the ground.

Goldie-Ox liked to keep fit, so every morning she raised the drawbridge twenty times. After that, to cool down, she swam around the moat and wrestled with the crocodile her father had given her for her last birthday.

Goldie-Ox let down the drawbridge with a soft thud. But wrestling with the crocodile wasn't fun any more. Nowadays he hid in the water weed as soon as she jumped in.

Goldie-Ox sighed. It was all Wolverina's fault. She had trained him to catch hard-boiled eggs and roll over for bits of bacon rind. And, of course, he much preferred doing that since he always lost wrestling with Goldie-Ox.

Goldie-Ox chewed on one of the sunflowers that grew beside the drawbridge. It wasn't that she really minded about the crocodile. On the whole, she was pretty easy-going.

It was just that Goldie-Ox knew perfectly well that Wolverina had only done it to annoy her. That was what Wolverina was like.

Goldie-Ox frowned. What was it Crotchet had called Wolverina? A mangy old dog. No. That couldn't be right. Crotchet was their nanny, but she would never have called Wolverina such a name. Not out loud, anyway.

A dog in the manger! That was it! Crotchet was right. Wolverina was a dog in a manger. She wanted everything for herself.

And that included the whole kingdom, ever since their father had said he was going to retire to the seaside.

Goldie-Ox spat out the prickly stalk and drop-kicked the sunflower into the moat.

At that moment, an extraordinary-looking frog leapt out of the moat. It had bright blue eyes and a tiny black stick tucked under its arm.

Goldie-Ox watched in amazement as the frog pulled out a gold pocket-watch and peered at it.

*Whap!*

A pebble flashed out of nowhere and hit the frog on the eye.

'Gotcha!' cackled a nasty voice from above. 'Slimy great toad! Next time I'll feed you to my crocodile!'

Goldie-Ox looked up. Wolverina was hanging like a bat from a branch above her.

'He's not your crocodile, he's my crocodile,' said Goldie-Ox, patiently. 'And that was no ordinary frog you clobbered, either.'

'Toads, frogs. Who cares?' Wolverina jumped to the ground. 'Besides, he was swimming in my moat.'

'Don't start that again,' said Goldie-Ox. She took a deep breath. 'What do you want to do today?'

'Let's catch snakes!' shouted Wolverina. 'I order you!'

Goldie-Ox shuddered. 'No!'

Last week, Wolverina had wound eight snakes into a necklace. She had trained them not to wriggle until the moment when she and Goldie-Ox sat down to tea with Crotchet.

Poor Crotchet. She nearly choked on her buttered scone, and had to be carried to bed.

'It's my turn to choose what we do,' said Goldie-Ox. 'And we haven't ...'

'... taken a rotten picnic and camped in a stinking tent for ages,' sneered Wolverina. She had guessed exactly what Goldie-Ox had in mind.

'That's not fair and you know it,' cried Goldie-Ox.

'A queen can do anything she wants,' smirked Wolverina.

A trumpet blast shook the air.

Grizzle strode across the lawn. He was dressed in his official pink and gold bell-bottomed trousers.

'King Codger orders the Ladies Goldie-Ox and Wolverina to come to the great hall,' he cried. 'The future of the kingdom is to be settled once and for all.'

# 3

# The quest for the Golden See-Saw

'Are you sure it will work?' whispered King Codger.

'Of course it will work,' snapped Spangle. He put a rusty old kettle over the fire. 'It's magic, isn't it?'

'Looks like a piece of junk to me,'
muttered King Codger. 'By the way,
where did you get that black eye?'

'Somebody threw a stone at me,'
replied Spangle, in such a voice that
King Codger knew not to ask any more.

A thin wisp of steam began to rise
from the kettle's spout.

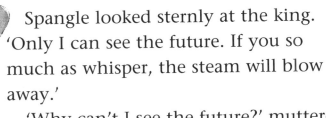

Spangle looked sternly at the king. 'Only I can see the future. If you so much as whisper, the steam will blow away.'

'Why can't I see the future?' muttered King Codger.

'Because you're a king and I'm a magician.' Spangle rolled his eyes. 'All right?'

King Codger pulled a face. He began to pull the furry bits out of his leopardskin cuffs.

A moment later the wisp of steam formed a perfect square. Spangle put his finger to his lips and peered into it. It was as if he was watching a moving picture.

'Of course!' he shouted. 'Why didn't I think of that?'

'Think of what?' snapped King Codger.

Spangle beamed and bowed low. 'Sire, your bad dreams are over.'

'Not if I haven't got what I want,' shrieked Wolverina from the door.

Spangle spun round. He held his arms high. The folds of his long sparkling cloak were like two huge wings.

'The future of the kingdom has been decided!' he roared. 'The Lady Goldie-Ox and the Lady Wolverina must go on a quest.' He glared at Wolverina. 'At once!'

'I'm not going on any stupid quests,' yelled Wolverina.

'Oh yes you are!' said Spangle. 'You will seek the Golden See-Saw.'

Goldie-Ox looked puzzled. 'What's a see-saw?'

'It's something that only works when two people play together,' explained Grizzle, kindly.

Oh, thought Goldie-Ox. No wonder I didn't know.

'I'm not playing on any stupid see-saws,' yelled Wolverina.

There was a clap of thunder and sparks shot out from Spangle's fingers.

'You have twenty-one days to bring back the Golden See-Saw,' ordered Spangle. 'If you fail, the kingdom of King Codger shall be ruled by your cousin, Cedric the Soppy.'

You could have heard a goblin sniff.

'Cedric the Soppy?' whispered
Goldie-Ox.

'Cedric the Soppy?' yelled Wolverina.

Goldie-Ox and Wolverina looked at
each other, horrified. This was the worst
news in the world.

Cedric the Soppy pressed flowers and painted pictures by numbers. The thought of him becoming king …

'Well?' said Spangle, crossing his arms.

Wolverina glared at him. Her golden snake-eyes glittered with fury.

'All right, you pointy-hatted creep,' she muttered. 'I'll go.'

# 4

# A handful of berries

For twenty days Goldie-Ox and
Wolverina followed windy paths through
forests, climbed rocky mountains and
waded through swamps.

They were dirty, hungry and tired.

Wolverina stared at the ragged edges of her favourite black jacket. She looked down at her precious green boots. They were ripped and torn.

Wolverina felt like screaming. She felt like running straight back home and kicking the first thing she saw.

But she didn't. She clenched her teeth and kept on going. The thought of Cedric the Soppy and his paintings by numbers was too terrible.

'I should have hit him with a rock,'
muttered Wolverina. They were
stumbling through yet another dark
forest.

It was the last day of their quest. Not
once had they seen anything that
looked like a see-saw, let alone a golden
one. But Goldie-Ox never complained.
That made it worse.

'Hit who?' asked Goldie-Ox as she
gathered berries.

'Spangle, of course,' muttered Wolverina. 'Golden See-Saw! I bet it's a load of codswallop.'

Goldie-Ox swallowed hard. 'What about ...'

'Cousin Cedric?' cried Wolverina. 'He's a load of codswallop too.'

Goldie-Ox swallowed again.

'Maybe you're right.'

Wolverina stood with her mouth open. 'You mean – you agree with me?'

Something snapped inside Goldie-Ox.

All her strength, all her kindness, all her patience ran out like water down a plug hole. She slumped against a tree and her huge blonde head hung between her knees. She felt enormous, empty and helpless.

'What if I do?' she said in a flat voice. 'What difference is it going to make now?' With a bad-tempered flick of her hand, she threw away the berries they were going to eat for lunch.

Wolverina stared. She was completely amazed.

This wasn't how things were supposed to be at all. *She* was the one who did things like throwing away other people's lunch.

A horrible, sick feeling spread across Wolverina's stomach. It was as if the ground she stood on had turned to quicksand.

She bit her lip and picked up some of
the berries. 'Eat these,' she whispered.
She pushed a clumsy handful towards
her sister. 'They'll make you feel better.'

'Nothing will make me feel better.'

The sick feeling in Wolverina's
stomach got worse and worse. For the
first time in her life, she felt scared.

'Please don't give up,' she cried, in
a cracked voice. 'I – I've got a plan!'

'Your plans are always rotten.'

'This one's not!' sobbed Wolverina. Desperately, she tried to think of a plan. Then she saw the tree!

It was taller than any of the others and its branches started high up.

'Help me up that tree,' pleaded Wolverina. 'If there's a Golden See-Saw anywhere around, I'll see it.'

TOILE
10 k

But Goldie-Ox didn't move. 'The Golden See-Saw's a load of codswallop,' she muttered. 'You said so yourself.'

That did it.

Wolverina burst into tears. 'I was making it up,' she sobbed. 'I make everything up because, because ...' Wolverina hid her face in her hands, 'because nobody likes me.'

Goldie-Ox lifted up her huge head. Wolverina was huddled beside her like a crumpled paper bag. She watched as her sister's small hand moved across the ground. It crept under her own thick, strong fingers.

'I'm sorry, Goldie-Ox,' whispered a voice that didn't sound like Wolverina at all. 'This is all my fault. If I hadn't been so nasty ...'

Goldie-Ox swallowed, and felt her own eyes begin to prickle. But she couldn't think of anything to say. She was so used to the old Wolverina that the new Wolverina made her feel shy and tongue-tied.

She gave Wolverina's arm a tiny squeeze. Then she stood up and cupped her great hands. 'Up you go,' she said in a gruff voice. 'We'll beat cousin Cedric yet.'

45

# 5

# Doing the crocodile walk

The sun was setting when Goldie-Ox
and Wolverina reached the edge of the
dark, murky lake.

In the middle of the lake was an
island fringed with bulrushes and blue
and yellow irises.

And in the middle of that island was
the Golden See-Saw. Wolverina had seen
it from the top of the tall tree.

Goldie-Ox stared at the evil-looking, dark water. It was full of crocodiles.

And they weren't the kind that caught hard-boiled eggs and rolled over for bits of bacon.

Far away, the sky was turning red and orange and the sun was beginning to disappear.

'We'll never get to the Golden See-Saw in time,' cried Goldie-Ox.

'Yes, we will,' replied Wolverina, firmly. 'Can you split a log in half?'

Goldie-Ox pulled out the huge axe that hung from her belt. Five minutes later, she had finished making a tiny dug-out canoe.

'Are you sure this is going to work?' asked Goldie-Ox.

'It's our only chance,' said Wolverina. 'When I give the signal, run for it.'

Goldie-Ox frowned. 'Be careful,' she said. 'They look rather hungry.'

'Don't worry about me.' Wolverina grinned. 'I have a way with crocodiles.'

With that, Wolverina paddled out into the lake and began to hum a tune. It was a strange tune. It sounded slimy-scaly and fishy-tasty at the same time.

The crocodiles loved it.

One by one, they lined up behind Wolverina and followed her through the water.

Wolverina led them round the island, through the bulrushes, and back along the shore. Then she turned in front of Goldie-Ox and led the crocodiles towards the island.

A moment later, a straight line of scaly crocodile backs appeared in front of Goldie-Ox's feet.

'Now!' sang Wolverina in her fishy-slimy voice.

Goldie-Ox couldn't believe what she was about to do! She took a deep breath and bounded from back to back across the dark, murky water to the shore.

And there it was!

'It's b-e-a-u-t-i-f-u-l,' whispered Wolverina. She ran her hand along the smooth golden side of the See-Saw. 'How do you think it works?'

Goldie-Ox stood at one end and pushed the Golden See-Saw up and down. It was quite fun. But not as much as she was expecting.

'Maybe you stand at one end and walk down to the other?'

So they tried that.

It was fun, but not that much fun.

Goldie-Ox shook her head. What had Grizzle said?

*It's something that only works when two people play together.*

'Maybe we have to sit on it,' she said.

'I know!' cried Wolverina. 'You sit at one end and I sit at the other.'

'Which way do we face?'

Wolverina wasn't sure about that bit. 'Let's face each other,' she said with a quick smile.

And so Goldie-Ox and Wolverina climbed on either end of the Golden See-Saw.

It didn't matter that one was heavy and the other was light. There was something magic about the Golden See-Saw. It worked no matter who sat on it.

Goldie-Ox and Wolverina soared through the air. Up and down. Up and down. Up and down.

For the first time ever, they were playing together.

And it was brilliant!

# 6

# It's all in the steam

'Good gracious,' muttered King Codger.
He was looking out of his bedroom
window. 'Grizzle! What do you make of
this?'

Grizzle looked out.

Then he dropped the purple leather shoe he was polishing.

The Lady Goldie-Ox and the Lady Wolverina were playing on a see-saw. It looked as if they didn't have a care in the world.

'Grizzle,' whispered the king, as if he was scared somebody might hear. 'Do you think it will last?'

'How should I know?' replied Grizzle, crossly. 'Call for Spangle. He's the magician. He's supposed to know everything.'

A few minutes later there was a *plop* and a *squelch*. A frog with bright blue eyes hopped into the room. It pulled out a gold pocket-watch and peered at it.

'Sorry,' muttered Spangle, 'there was this princess, and, uh ...'

Grizzle glared at him and picked up the purple shoe. 'There *are* other fairy stories, you know,' he muttered.

Spangle coughed and turned himself back into a magician. 'Sire,' he murmured, bowing low to hide his red face. 'Why did you call for me?'

The sound of happy laughter floated in through the window.

'That's why,' said King Codger pointing outside.

'Well, knock me down with a pointy-hat,' cried Spangle, as he looked out of the window. 'It's worked!'

'Does this mean Wolverina will share the castle with her sister?' asked King Codger, slowly.

'Happily,' replied Spangle with a grin.
'And I can move to the seaside?'
'Any time.'
King Codger turned and stared at
Spangle's bright blue eyes. 'How long
will it last?' he asked.

Spangle held up his hands. The folds of his long, sparkling cloak flapped like two huge wings.

'Forever!'

King Codger looked down at the wild sunflowers that grew by the drawbridge. He looked up at the great stone walls of the castle. And he looked across the sunny, yellow fields, full of ripe corn, to the green hills beyond.

An extraordinary thought flashed through his mind. He didn't want to retire to the seaside at all – not now that Wolverina was happy and she and Goldie-Ox were friends.

He wanted to stay right here with his own family, in his own castle.

'And so you shall,' cried Spangle, reading the king's mind. 'It was written in the steam.'

He pulled out his golden pocket watch.

'Now, if you'll excuse me, I …'

But King Codger wasn't listening. He was dancing around the room as if he had jumping beans in his trousers.

'Grizzle!' he cried. 'Call for the Ladies Goldie-Ox and Wolverina! The future of the kingdom has been decided. We're all going to live happily ever after!'

# *About the author*

I was born in Canada and grew up in a log cabin. I spent my childhood messing about on the river in the backwoods of Quebec.

I have written over sixty children's books. I like writing funny books because I get to laugh at my own jokes.

Making up exactly the right names for characters is very important to me. Only then do they really come to life. Goldie-Ox and Wolverina are two of my favourites.